COTSWOLD
MOODS

Archie Miles

HALSGROVE

First published in Great Britain in 2003

Copyright © 2003 Archie Miles

British Library Cataloguing-in-Publication Data
A CIP record for this title is available from the British Library

ISBN 1 84114 265 4

HALSGROVE
Halsgrove House
Lower Moor Way
Tiverton, Devon EX16 6SS
Tel: 01884 243242
Fax: 01884 243325
email: sales@halsgrove.com
website: www.halsgrove.com

Printed and bound in Spain

INTRODUCTION

Living in the Cotswolds was marvellous but, like many of life's experiences, only when it's over do you begin to truly appreciate what exactly was so special. Coming back to somewhere I once called home is a meeting of mixed emotions: joy in the familiarity of old haunts, yet dismay at some of the changes wrought by commercialisation and development. Still, life goes on, and it certainly isn't healthy to insist that anywhere should remain locked in some personally-defined time warp. If many landscape photograpers had their way, most rural communities would be deprived of their electricity and telephones.

That the Cotswolds rely heavily on tourism is undeniable, and even more so in an era when the agricultural economy seems to be struggling, so I can temper my personal demands for peace and solitude with the rationale of objectivity. 'A weekend break in the Cotswolds' sounds great; and the reality for the visitor almost always lives up to the promise (great British weather permitting), but for the indigenous population it sometimes presents something of a compromise. The revenue from tourism is welcome, but does every-one have to head for the same honeypots in the height of summer? That rural retreat can risk becoming a sideshow in a theme park, so it would make simple common sense to spread the weight of tourism a little more evenly. Of course everyone is welcome in the Cotswolds, and weekenders, second-homers, incomers and locals alike combine to make a vibrant though fluctuating community.

So it transpired that when I was actively photographing in the Cotswolds, during my eight year sojourn, I tended to find most inspiration from the times of year or day when people were seldom in view. Landscape photographers often insist that the pursuit of their prey is very much a solitary affair, and although this sounds a little antisocial it gave me the time and space to create a very personal image of the Cotswolds, its land and its light, throughout the seasons.

The physical boundaries of the Cotswolds are quite difficult to define, although being the country's largest AONB, borders have been set. As a region, it is most readily identified by its architecture, rather than the landscape, and most particularly by the mellow and subtly-varied hues of the locally-quarried limestone. Some would suggest that the Cotswolds stretch as far south as Bath, and certainly the handsome dressed stone façades of that city would be compatible, yet the crux of *my* Cotswolds revolves around its noted market towns such as Chipping Campden and Moreton-in-Marsh, Stow-on-the-Wold and Chipping Norton, and all the Bs: Burford, Broadway and Bourton-on-the-Water. The evolution of these settlements and the history of prosperity in the region, certainly until the mid-nineteenth century, was built upon one thing. Wool.

Wool, its production, and the processes and industries that worked it, account for the Cotswolds known and loved by the thousands who live there and the millions who visit every year. Today that seems difficult to comprehend, for while sheep may still dot the landscape here and there, they are no longer the main thrust of the agricultural economy.

From the medieval period onwards, records abound of the prodigious trade both at home and abroad fired by the thriving Cotswold wool industry. For hundreds of years the patterns of the landscape were moulded by sheep farming – great tracts of pasture delineated by stone walls, a network of drovers' roads, innumerable barns to protect stock in winter and all their accompanying farmsteads. During the seventeenth and eighteenth centuries, as world trade expanded, the revenue from wool became one of Britain's principal sources of income, while the Crown also benefitted substantially from the tax upon it. Vast wealth accumulated by landowners and merchants funded some of the great houses of the region as well as the expansion of the towns, frequently assisted by benefactions from the great and the good either for the spiritual wellbeing of the community, manifested in some of the splendid churches, providing schools, estate cottages for their workers, or provision for the less fortunate in almshouses.

With the Industrial Revolution, the Age of The Golden Fleece rapidly ground to a halt. Competition from abroad and, more immediately, from the highly mechanised cloth producers in northern England, led to a drastically reduced demand for local wool and a collapse of the cloth industry. For almost a century the economy of the Cotswolds simply marked time until, in the latter half of the twentieth century, tourism grew and began to discover and exploit such unspoilt rural gems.

Although many Cotswold villages may have remained little altered over the last hundred years there has been a marked change in the appearance of the landscape. Far across the undulating hills, the sheep have dwindled in number and the network of fine stone walls, which once harboured them, has been rationalised into great sprawling enclosures for wheat or oilseed rape. Some splendid ancient woodlands still survive along the western scarp of the Cotswolds, yet to the east much has been lost in favour of arable use or softwood plantations. This doesn't necessarily signal a change for the worse, but it is different.

Defining exactly what makes the Cotswolds a special place for me is not hard, though by many people's standards it may seem obscure. Sure, the villages like Upper and Lower Slaughter are pretty, and tourist haunts of Bourton or Broadway have their charm, but it's that perfect harmony built from all the tiniest and often barely perceived elements that make my Cotswolds. The fleeting effects of light and shade on the land, or the drama of a skyscape never to be repeated. The textures of earth, stone, tree bark or flower petal. The graphic shapes of walls, barns and stark trees against brooding skies. The mystery of misty mornings. The ringing clarity of a hoar-frosted winter's day. The first rays of sun at daybreak, flexing fingers across the land, defining the contours. Rugged moss-clad stone-slated rooftops, set higgledy-piggledy through some tranquil village. The honey glow at day's end of a cottage set squarely in its rightful place, accustomed and made comfortable by the centuries. And, of course, so much more...

I believe that seeking pictures is like digging for treasure; the subjects are often buried just beneath the surface, and it needs a keen eye, an open mind and a measure of good fortune to bring forth the gems. While this is a very personal view of the Cotswolds, I hope it is one that will touch other people's sense of this magical place.

ARCHIE MILES, 2003

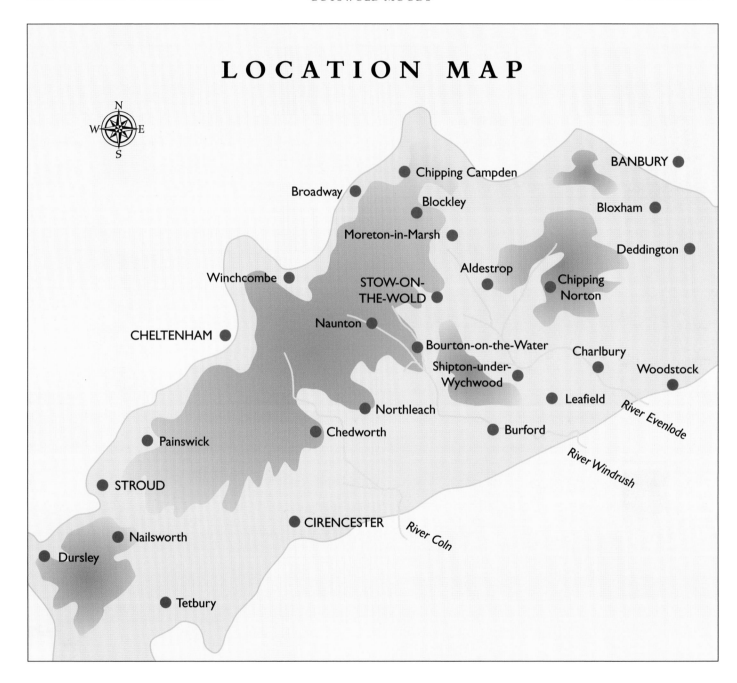

LOCATION MAP

BANBURY

Chipping Campden

Broadway

Blockley

Bloxham

Moreton-in-Marsh

Deddington

Aldestrop

Winchcombe

STOW-ON-THE-WOLD

Chipping Norton

Naunton

CHELTENHAM

Bourton-on-the-Water

Charlbury

Woodstock

Shipton-under-Wychwood

Northleach

Leafield

River Evenlode

Chedworth

Burford

Painswick

River Windrush

STROUD

CIRENCESTER

River Coln

Nailsworth

Dursley

Tetbury

Green lanes, drovers' roads and half forgotten trackways criss-cross the Cotswold landscape Once the highways of agricultural trade, most are now reduced to the status of paths and bridleways which provide an excellent network for walkers and riders.

The town of Chipping Campden is notable for its fine array of Cotswold vernacular architecture, with numerous variations from the medieval through to the Revival Movement of the last century, yet all built from the distinctive honey-coloured local stone. The town's original prosperity grew out of the wool trade, and the epicentre of commercial activity was the Market Hall, from which this view is taken. Built in 1627, it was given to the town by Sir Baptist Hicks.

Early morning over the rooftops of Chipping Campden.

This older style road sign at Broadwell points the way to three of the region's small market towns – Stow, Moreton and Chipping Norton – 00as well as the village of Adlestrop, immortalised by the poet Edward Thomas. It has been replaced by a modern printed metal sign, on which some of these settlements have mysteriously moved. Evenlode is now 2, Moreton is 4 and Chipping Norton is 8 miles distant.

Taking on the mantle of a naturalistic, albeit man-moulded, waymarker these 'knotted' trees at (most appropriately) Notgrove are common limes – although the village name most probably derives from nut grove, implying the presence of hazel. These trees may look strange, but are perfectly healthy, the 'knots' simply forming as a result of regular pruning at the same points.

A barn between Notgrove and Turkdean, protected by a fine stand of beech trees.

Frost still hangs in the hollows on a November morning near Turkdean.

A bitterly cold morning in a Cotswold wood, every bough and blade etched with ice.

Early winter morning along an old trackway through Foxholes Wood, near Lyneham. As the sun penetrates, a continual cascade of ice falls from the trees, accompanying the muffled footfall of the lone explorer.

Ancient oak coppice stool in Lineover Wood, above Dowdeswell Reservoir. This tree is probably several hundred years old, but due to regular harvesting of poles has remained healthy and productive, as well as providing habitat for ferns, lichens and mosses. These hoary old veterans should be treasured and carefully managed as they represent a vital element of our green heritage.

Early morning burst of autumnal sunshine in Lineover Wood.

A beech clump above Condicote on a bleak winter's day.

Squire's Clump, a splendid group of beeches above an ancient burial mound near Sarsden.

A cluster of cottages in Lower Turkdean.

Two different barn ends, one with a dovecote above. Barns used as barns in the Cotswolds are becoming a rare commodity, as many are snapped up and converted into bijou country homes.

Wintery chocolate-box cottage in Kingham.

A mirror provided for safe access in Kingham offers an unusual view of the village.

Cattle snorting and munching their way through winter fodder on the hills above Icomb.

Sheep may safely graze around this smallholding near Northleach.

A farmer brings his cows in for milking in the chill of winter.

Low evening sunlight glances across medieval ridge-and-furrow patterns near Adlestrop. The reversed S-shaped pattern of the middle distance field is typical of the older formation of ridge-and-furrow, probably medieval or earlier, when large teams of oxen were used for ploughing. Somewhat ungainly to manage, these beasts required a large turning space at the end of the field, and so it was necessary to begin the turn well before the headland. The more recent straight ridge-and-furrow usually indicates the use of horse-drawn ploughs.

Great open tracts of arable land now dominate much of the Cotswolds. Love it or loathe it, oilseed rape is here to stay and in recent years, depending on how the subsidies prevail, vast swathes of land have submitted to the vivid yellow blanket.

Ploughing near Chedworth.

Winter frosts grip the fields of the Windrush Valley.

Derelict barn near Great Barrington. Since the photograph was taken this has become a handsome home.

Springtime in Maughersbury.

Cotswold stone abounds, traditionally quarried from numerous different sites; the expert eye can place individual building stones or roof tiles to their hole in the ground. The village well at Wyck Rissington (left) may once have refreshed the villages, but now its finely-dressed blocks perform as a rather grand flower tub, while the old stones of the Norman church of St Andrew at Chedworth have told the time for centuries.

The Rollright Stones, near Chipping Norton, a Bronze Age circle of some 70 standing stones set in a 100 foot diameter circle (of which this is but one part). Known as The King's Men, legend has it that this is a marrauding king with his army who, in the mists of time, once threatened the region. Stopped in their tracks by a powerful witch, they were all turned to stone.

The Devil's Chimney, high on Leckhampton Hill above Cheltenham, was left behind when the nearby quarries were abandoned. It is the local belief that the 'chimney' rises straight from Hell.

Ducks aplenty at Chedworth.

Early morning view across a bend in the River Evenlode.

Grey and sinuous ashes amidst the morning mists of the Dikler valley near Lower Swell.

Glorious sunset over Stow-on-the-Wold.

Twice a year, in May and October, Romanies the length and breadth of Britain head for the horse fairs at Stow-on-the-Wold, to which they have been coming for more than five hundred years. These gatherings are not just for the buying and selling of horses, but also for trading all manner of merchandise. Recreation, gambling, socialising and even such special events as Romany weddings are reserved for these dates in the calendar. It's an excuse to don one's finery, as this striking young woman (with her son) has done, trade a pony or two, and put a lick of paint on the old caravan.

Summer's evening over the hamlet of Chilson, and the lazy smoke of a bonfire drifts down the valley.

A field full of poppies, a rare sight since the advent of herbicides which have denuded pastures and crops alike of the splendid arrays of wild flowers once so familiar to our forebears. Yet sometimes seeds may lie in the earth for many years until the conditions are favourable enough for them to spring anew, as these poppies have done.

A few corners of fields, ditches and forgotten woodlands have remained refuges for wild flowers, and here a carpet of snowdrops briefly overwhelms the plough.

Detail of an old barn at Lower Oddington, latterly converted to a pair of houses. The triangular ventilation holes are now functioning as extremely small and unusual windows.

Winter comes to the village of Calcot in the Coln valley.

After the snow and a long wet spell, the River Coln bursts its banks at Calcot.

The Saxon church of St Andrew at Coln Rogers peers over the wall at the approaching flood waters.

Sunset along the Evenlode valley near Kingham.

An alleyway behind a Winchcombe pub, and flower-decked cottages in the town.

View from Belas Knap, a 4000 year old long barrow, down into the Isbourne valley, with Sudeley Castle in the distance. There has been a castle here since Saxon times, but the existing building is largely fifteenth century with sixteenth century additions. One of its most famous occupants was Katherine Parr, Henry VIII's widow. A Royalist stronghold during the Civil War, it was captured by the Parliamentarian forces and deliberately ruined, and it remained thus for almost 200 years until the Dent family, who still own it, bought it in 1837 and began a lengthy restoration process which took almost a hundred years to complete.

View down the Painswick valley from hills above Wick Street.

The small town of Painswick overlooks the valley of the Painswick Brook. Another of Gloucestershire's fine wool towns, the architecture dates largely from the seventeenth and eighteenth centuries. Here the sun briefly illuminates the valley on one of those gusty November days.

Early morning down the Windrush valley near Naunton.

Evening glow above a Maughersbury skyline.

Winter in the Windrush valley at Burford, where recently pollarded willows dot the water meadows.

Several years later, one of the same trees shows the resulting collapse of boughs which have ceased to be managed. Pollarding is a regime which should be maintained once initiated.

The church of St John the Baptist in Burford is an attractive building incorporating numerous styles and additions. But it is perhaps most remarkable for its outstanding collection of tombstones; some of which are fashioned in the shape of bales of wool denoting the last resting places of the wealthy wool merchants of this medieval town. Some of the details are a bit spooky!

Spring morning in Burford High Street.

A pair of remarkable survivors. Since the onslaught of Dutch elm disease in the 1970s, almost every mature English elm has disappeared from the British landscape, but miraculously these two fine examples have survived at Upper Swell.

There are several arboreta across the Cotswolds, but arguably the best of the bunch is Westonbirt, near Tetbury. Tree planting began in 1829, and for more than a hundred years members of the Holford family created this outstanding collection of trees from around the world. Upon the demise of the last family member the estate passed to the Crown in lieu of death duties and since 1956, it has been in the care of the Forestry Commission. There are some 4000 different species of trees and shrubs set in 600 acres, and so there is always plenty to see at any time of year.

The outstanding displays of maples at Westonbirt make an autumn visit essential. The vivid red *Acer palmatum* and the varied hues of *Acer griseum* are but two of a huge collection.

A chance discovery of this group of coppiced small-leaved limes in Silk Wood, at Westonbirt, a few years ago didn't immediately seem particularly exciting, but further investigation with the aid of DNA fingerprinting revealed that they were all part of the same tree. Remarkably, all of these were a single coppiced lime stool and it is currently estimated to be in excess of 2000 years old. It is a great stroke of good fortune that it was not grubbed out during the planting of the arboretum.

Trees have great presence when alive and sometimes even after they have died. This crusty old sentinel oak guards a pair of cottages at Barnsley.

Roots and stumps create their own fascinations.

The church of St Peter at Little Barrington with one of its lichen encrusted gravestones. It was stone from the Barrington quarries which was used to build St Paul's Cathedral in London, as well as many other Wren churches in the city.

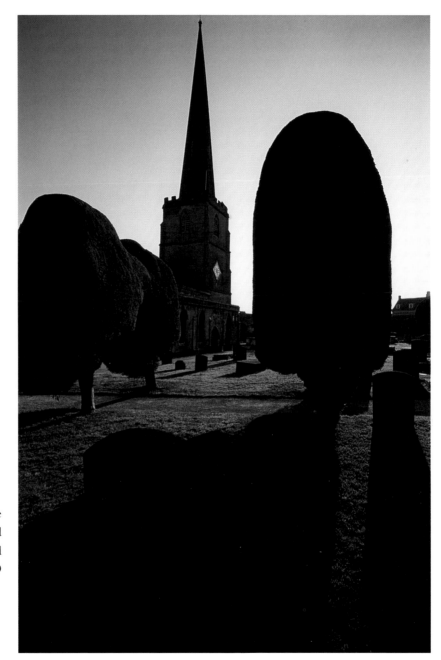

In complete contrast with Little Barrington is the graceful spire and immaculately manicured churchyard of St Mary's in Painswick, with its 99 yew trees trimmed to perfection.

The tiny church of St Michael at Duntisbourne Rouse perches on the valley side.

A bright crisp winter's day at Duntisbourne Rouse.

A thatched cricket pavilion perched on staddle-stones at Stanway, designed by J.M. Barrie, who was a frequent visitor to the village and a cricket enthusiast. Traditionally barns used as grain stores were built on staddle-stones to keep the contents dry and to protect them from rats.

The village of Stanway set snugly beneath the western scarp of the Cotswolds.

Blockley is right on the cusp of being a small town or large village, but was yet another community largely built around the wool trade. Various water-powered mills along the Knee Brook once processed the wool although in the late seventeenth century, a small yet successful silk industry evolved which promised greater profits. A claim to fame is that the village was the first in England to be lit by electricity, back in 1887, when one of the old water mills was converted for the purpose.

Early morning flock near Guiting Power.

The village of Naunton, set in the Upper Windrush valley.

Morning mists rise slowly near Naunton.

When snow sweeps across the exposed tops of the Cotswolds there is frequently only an inch or two on the fields, but where drifts build up against walls it can make roads totally impassable.

Hoar-frosted white willows in the Evenlode valley.

Cattle on a chilly morning near Icomb.

An ancient sweet chestnut bowed by many a gale still sits resolutely on the hills above Snowshill.

Snowshill Manor, now owned by the National Trust, is a Cotswold tourist honeypot. Owned by the architect cum eclectic collector Charles Paget Wade, between 1919 and 1951, this Tudor house is stuffed to the rafters with all manner of fascinating things; such as clocks, musical instruments, bicycles, dolls' houses, puppets, and even an awesome collection of Samurai armour, which is exhibited on ferocious looking manikins set in an eerie half light. Did one just move? The gardens are extensive and full of interest, such as this statue of George and the Dragon, carved in 1922.

The village of Snowshill from Oat Hill.

Broadway is another great magnet for tourists, but now the constant roar of passing traffic has been greatly reduced by the opening of a bypass. Soft evening light brings out the mellow tones of the stone.

View from hills above Broadway out towards the Vale of Evesham.

Early morning at the tiny hamlet of Cutsdean.

A blanket of snow lies deep across the churchyard of St Andrew's in Kingham.

Chill February morning walk along the River Eye at Lower Slaughter.

It may be winter, but these geese don't seem to notice the cold.

Lower Slaughter; a classic view of one of the Cotswold's prettiest villages – and a cat on a mission.

In the summer the same view glows in the late evening sunlight.

Out for a morning ride: crossing the River Eye at Upper Slaughter.

Spring morning over Lower Slaughter.

The Blenheim Orange (a.k.a. Blenheim Pippin, Woodstock Pippin and Kempster's Pippin) was a chance seedling discovered at Woodstock in 1818. Dubbed Blenheim in honour of the nearby seat of the Duke of Marlborough, this was once a much planted variety in Cotswold orchards.

A Blenheim Orange apple tree, at least a hundred years old, and now a rare survivor of a once prolific variety. Often called the Christmas Apple due to its excellent keeping.

The noble face of a shire horse mare at the Cotswold Farm Park near Guiting Power.

Details of a beautiful pair of gates at Barton-on-the-Heath are the work of a gifted local blacksmith. The towering pile of horseshoes is his pension fund!

A farmyard Jack Russell with attitude, at Broadwell.

The shaggy face of a Highland cow at the Cotswold Farm Park. Despite their appearance, they are one of the most docile of breeds.

Cattle roam across a vast open pasture on a misty morning near Shipston-on-Stour.

Horse in snowy field at Maughersbury.

A knot of stone walls behind a dilapidated farmstead above Stanway.

An Albertine rose cascades over a wall of limestone slabs; an unusual way to build a wall with stone, but a style found in and around many Cotswold villages.

Pretty in pink. The common spotted may be our commonest orchid, but this doesn't diminish its beauty. Ragged robin is a plant of damp places and now becoming quite scarce. The cuckooflower is also a lover of damp ground, whether it be verges, ditches or river banks; its name derives from the fact that when it blooms in April it frequently coincides with the first calls of the migrant bird.

Honeysuckle is a rambler of woodland and hedgerow alike, and most memorable for its intoxicating scent – particularly at night, when the plant attracts pollinating moths.

Morning sunlight along a trackway through Lineover Wood.

The previous day this Japanese cherry at Church Westcote stood resplendent in its autumn finery. In the night the frost came. The next day the mantle had become a carpet.

Shadows lengthen across the fields near Chastleton.

All over the Cotswolds the evidence of ancient ridge-and-furrow is a constant reminder of the agricultural past. Remarkably, even in fields which have been ploughed many times with modern practice, it is very difficult to eradicate the old patterns.

Outbuilding and Belfast sink at Great Barrington.

Estate workers' cottages at Great Barrington.

For some years the Barrington Estate was in a state of decline by dint of neglect, a process which has fortunately been reversed in recent times.

Well away from the period stone frontages of Bourton-on-the-Water, on the edge of the village, sat a remarkably fine corrugated iron home. Its replacement, a Cotswold stone house, is probably infinitely warmer in winter, cooler in summer, and certainly quieter in a rain storm.

Evening at Evenlode.

With the advent of massive steel-framed barns and plastic-wrapped round bales, the
sight of a haystack in a rickyard has all but disappeared.

Set apart from the main house at Chastleton is this quaint little dovecote.

Until 1991 when the National Trust acquired it, Chastleton House, a fine seventeenth century building which had been in the hands of the Jones family for almost four hundred years, was rapidly falling into serious disrepair. As with so many of these big old houses, the cost of upkeep was becoming prohibitive, but the Trust have turned things around, conserving the house as it stood upon acquisition, rather than undertaking total restoration, thus revealing a time capsule of life in a large country house.

Now lost in the mists (or smokescreens) of agricultural life is the tradition of burning off the stubble from arable crops. Although it is much better for the environment not to burn, it was an annual event which conjured up some interesting images.

Morning mist sweeps down the valley near Ascott–under–Wychwood.

Massive bole of an old beech tree on top of the Cotswolds.

Beech clumps and avenues are a frequent feature of the landscape. A shallow rooting tree, beech still seems to find great purchase in the rocky, lime-rich soils, even in quite exposed locations.

Handsome farmhouse near the village pond in Wyck Rissington.

The village pond at Chedworth.

Frosty spring morning in Fifield.

The village pub is still often the epicentre of village life, although one of the smallest must be The Plough Inn at Kelmscot.

Winter wheat shoots forth in the Windrush valley, near Sherborne.

The village of Sherborne.

Heavy hoar frost near Ascott-under-Wychwood touches oaks which were once part of a hedgerow.

Misty morning above Ascott-under-Wychwood.

Horse chestnut finds its place in our parks and gardens principally for its splendid display of creamy white candles each June. This typically shaped specimen is in a pasture near Stanway.

Autumnal lane in Idbury.

Grove of springtime poplars in a plantation at Salperton.

Grove of winter poplars in a plantation at Bruern.

Blue anemones are the naturalised European cousins of our native wood anemone, that reliable indicator of ancient woodland. These flowers in Oddington Woods must have been planted a long time ago to have achieved such coverage.

An impressive coppiced field maple in Lineover Wood. The name derives from the Saxon *Lindofer* indicating a bank of lime trees, and several fine examples still grow there.

Old signpost in Chipping Campden.

As night falls, Broadway Tower stands boldly on the skyline.

An almost totally man-made landscape viewed from the Fosse Way near Turkdean. Man has created bigger fields to accomodate his massive machinery, and planted great swathes of fast-growing softwoods. What did this view look like when the Romans forged their main highway here some 2000 years ago?

Misty morning off the eastern edge of the Cotswolds near Westcote.

The village of Condicote.

The Four Shires Stone near Moreton-in-Marsh, a reminder of the days when this was the meeting point of the Oxfordshire, Gloucestershire, Worcestershire and Warwickshire borders. It is absolutely covered in graffiti.

Misty evening over Stow Hill.

Early morning on a bend in the River Evenlode.

Field barn tucked in a hollow of the hills near Notgrove.

Sunset through an old ash tree near Chastleton.

Rainbow over Churchill.